— **Spiritual Seekers who live in the modern world need to read this book!**

"If you are looking to be "awake in the market place" it is essential to understand the development of our reliance on science as the arbiter of truth. As our perspectives shift toward the inclusion of quantum theory, we benefit from those that have done the hard work to put words to that shift and how it includes spirituality. I've read a fair amount of books on quantum theory and on spirituality and I have struggled with the concepts and the complexities of both, but reading this book by Jeff Carreira was enjoyable. I felt like I was sitting on a park bench with a dear friend who was happily recounting a personal journey of deep understanding. Jeff Carreira has an integrated knowledge of the relationship of science, spirituality and quantum theory that allows for elegant simplicity. His writing leaves room for my imagination to participate in the development of his ideas and there is kindness implicit in his wording that calms the readers mind as these vast ideas dance across the pages. I've read it a few times now and have found gems of insight each passage through the book. It feels like this is an introduction to a much larger body of work ahead and I look forward to reading more of his writing."

— Necessary Reading to Preserve Humanity's Future

"This short, simple, but DEEPLY important book explains why we need to open up our minds to question what our inherited assumptions are that are keeping us stuck and we need it Now. A quick and engaging summary of what Jeff Carreira has been studying for years, I find it compelling to apply it to every facet of current life to transcend our outdated thinking that got us into trouble here today. Einstein is often quoted for the idea that we cannot solve a problem from the level of thinking that created it, and this book takes us to the next step. We can save ourselves, but we need this shift in our thinking to do it before it's too late."

— Highly Recommended...

"Despite the words "quantum physics" in its title, this is a book for nearly everyone. Jeff Carreira has made complex material easy, exciting, and a pleasure to read. He reminds us that even though key discoveries of quantum physics are more than 100-years old, we are still living in the old worldview of classical physics, in the Cartesian-Newton paradigm. He suggests that by altering our worldview to include quantum theory, we might find solutions to our multiple planetary crises that we cannot see from the old worldview. He also makes a strong and valid point about how we have adopted scientism over science and our need to return to science. This short, uplifting, and intelligent book is so worth your time."

— **Jeff encourages the reader to let in and live what we already know**

"In this wonderful little book Jeff gives us a gentle but firm nudge to use our creativity to live in a way which reflects more fully our deepest understanding. He does this by first showing us how we continue, quite reasonably, to believe the evidence of our eyes in denial of clear evidence that has been around for over a century. Jeff does this in a way that makes nothing we do wrong but asks why it seems so preposterous to think of our universe in a radically different way. And what would happen if, as has already occurred twice in recent memory, there is a fundamental shift in how we view ourselves, our world and everything else."

— **A Real Joy**

"This book is simultaneously accessible and mind blowing. What could be more exciting than a book that causes one to re-frame and question perceptions of reality? The Spiritual Implications of Quantum Physics has important implications and deserves to be read thoughtfully to allow different facets to land internally. Having retained only the general gist of Thomas Kuhn's The Structure of Scientific Revolutions, I found it helpful to have the foundational material reviewed and framed in a relevant light. It's thrilling to be reminded that so many possibilities for "living potentials" are hiding in plain sight, if we only knew how to access them. This is the book that will help you see through new eyes."

Other Books in The Reflections Series:

Radical Inclusivity: Expanding Our Minds Beyond Dualistic Thinking by Jeff Carreira.

The Miracle of Self-Realization: Reflections on the Spiritual Teachings of Ramana Maharshi by Jeff Carreira

The Miracle of an Open Mind: Reflections on the Philosophy of William James by Jeff Carreira

Evolution, Intuition and Reincarnation: Reflections on the spiritual vision of Ralph Waldo Emerson by Jeff Carreira

The Power of Creative Flow: Reflections on Peak Performance, Cultural Transformation, and Spiritual Growth by Jeff Carreira

The Battle of Science and Spirituality: Reflections on the History of Western Philosophy by Jeff Carreira

Free Resources from Jeff Carreira

Life Without Fear: Meditation as an Antidote to Anxiety with Jeff Carreira. Visit lifewithoutfear.online

Secrets of Profound Meditation: Six Spiritual Insights that will Transform Your Life with Jeff Carreira. Visit secretsofprofoundmeditation.com

Foundations of a New Paradigm: A 6-part program designed to shift the way you experience everything with Jeff Carreira. Visit foundationsofanewparadigm.com

THE SPIRITUAL IMPLICATIONS OF QUANTUM PHYSICS:

Reflections on the Nature of Science, Reality and Paradigm Shifts

Copyright © 2023 by Jeff Carreira

All rights reserved. Except as permitted under U.S. Copyright Act of 1976, no part of this publication may be reproduced, distributed, or transmitted in any form or by any means, or stored in a database or retrieval system, without the prior written permission of the publisher.

ISBN: 978-1-954642-32-4

Emergence Education
P.O. Box 63767
Philadelphia, PA 19147
EmergenceEducation.com

Cover design by Silvia Rodrigues
Interior design by Sophie Peirce.

Printed in the United States of America.

THE SPIRITUAL IMPLICATIONS *of* QUANTUM PHYSICS

Reflections on

THE NATURE OF SCIENCE, REALITY
AND PARADIGM SHIFTS

JEFF CARREIRA

EMERGENCE EDUCATION
Philadelphia, Pennsylvannia

Contents

Introduction . . . . *xv*

01: Nothing Changes, but Everything's Different. 1

02: Do Time and Space Exist? 31

03: Has Consciousness Evolved?. 55

Selected Bibliography. *77*
About the Author *79*

JEFF CARREIRA

> *The more we delve into quantum mechanics the stranger the world becomes; appreciating this strangeness of the world, whilst still operating in that which you now consider reality, will be the foundation for shifting the current trajectory of your life from ordinary to extraordinary. It is the Tao of mixing this cosmic weirdness with the practical and physical, which will allow you to move, moment by moment, through parallel worlds to achieve your dreams.*

~ KEVIN MICHEL

Introduction

ABOUT A CENTURY AGO, a major revolution happened in the field of physics. Over the span of a few decades, relativity theory and quantum mechanics radically altered our fundamental view of reality.

That dramatic revolution captured the imaginations of countless individuals and many wonderful books have been written about it. Most of those books explain the science and tell us about the true nature of reality that it revealed. I have read a number of those books and loved them, but this is not one of those. When I started this project, I wondered what I had to add to the wealth of literature that already existed.

This book offers a very specific exploration. It's not about the science, although I will share some of that with you. It's also not about the new world that quantum physics has revealed, although I will speculate about that a bit too. What this book is really about is why, after nearly a century, the radical implications of the new physics have had so little impact on our everyday experience of reality.

We will explore how paradigms shift, or why they mostly don't. We will move slowly and carefully through an examination of how our perception of reality becomes embedded in our assumptions about it. We will see how the way we speak and think creates our experience, and why it's nearly impossible for us to see beyond what we believe is true.

I wrote this book as an opportunity and an invitation. It is an opportunity to open your heart and mind to a new reality, and an invitation to play a part in bringing that new reality to life.

Jeff Carreira

> *The 'paradox' is only a conflict between reality and your feeling of what reality 'ought to be'.*
>
> – RICHARD FEYNMAN

01

Nothing Changes, but Everything's Different

"Observations not only disturb what is to be measured, they produce it."

~ PASCUAL JORDAN

JEFF CARREIRA

During my high school years, I became a self-proclaimed atheist because I was compelled by the evidence-based understanding of the natural world that science offered. I majored in physics as an undergraduate because I was a scientific materialist who believed that reality was fundamentally a material place and so if I understood physics, I would understand the nature of reality.

In my senior year, I took a yearlong course in quantum physics. That course hammered the first big crack in my materialistic worldview. As I learned about the scientific community's struggle to understand what was happening at the atomic and subatomic level of our universe, I discovered something I was not expecting. Physicists are in many ways just making up stories about reality. They don't know what is ultimately going on. Science is very good at answering questions about what is happening, but not as good at understanding why it's happening.

At the time that I was studying in college, string

theory was gaining popularity as a way of understanding the bizarre world that physicists had uncovered. String theory to me sounded like a very elaborate story created to explain things. Could it be true that at the end of the day scientists were just storytellers too? I didn't find string theory to be any more appealing as an explanation of the nature of reality than the stories I had heard in church as a child. I started to suspect that science was not going to bring me the ultimate knowledge of reality that I longed for. Quantum mechanics was a difficult course for me to complete, but I managed to earn a passing grade and graduate. My faith in science had been weakened but was still fundamentally intact.

After graduation, I took a position as a research engineer in a fast-growing high-tech company that supplied laser diodes for the booming telecommunications industry of the 1980's. My loss of faith in science became complete during my tenure as an engineer. Over and over again I would see a whole team of truly brilliant scientists get lured down rabbit holes of wild speculation for months at a time. Once we emerged out the other end of the dark tunnels of speculative ideas, we would create a new theory and dive back in. Of course, along the way we made valuable discoveries and created new technologies, but over those years I began to wonder how much of our success was due to the accuracy of our understanding of reality, and how much was luck.

Developing and manufacturing laser diodes turned out to be a perfect background for philosophical investigation. The lasers we produced were small enough to fit in the jaws of an ant, but the actual working part of the laser was only a few atoms thick. The laser was essentially a microscopic sandwich made up of an active layer of metal surrounded on top and bottom by inactive layers. When electricity was applied across the active layer it became electrically excited and emitted light particles called photons. These photons would always be of exactly the same wavelength determined by the makeup of the active layer material.

You can probably imagine how difficult it is to really know what is going on in a laser that is only a few atoms thick. I sat through many meetings with the research team listening to creative and often brilliant speculations about what might be going on and why things might be working, or not working. Slowly I came to the conviction that we had no way of knowing what was really going on.

In the middle of all this, I came upon a book that became the last nail in the coffin of my scientific faith, *The Structure of Scientific Revolutions* by Thomas Kuhn. Kuhn had been a professor specializing in the history of science when he published this groundbreaking work in 1962. As I read the book, my eyes opened. In between the experimental facts that science adores and the ideas scientists write about them in books, there are layers of assumption and interpretation. This middle ground is the place where meaningless observations of phenomenon are clothed in speculations about their meaning and significance. It is where facts become theories about the facts. Much later I learned that this tendency to make up theories to explain what observed facts might be telling us about reality, was a habit that the famous Austrian scientist, Ernst Mach, had warned adamantly against at the turn of the last century.

Kuhn's book ignited an awakening in me that eventually led me away from the work of science and placed me squarely on a path of spiritual pursuit. *The Structure of Scientific Revolutions* is not a long book, but it is also not an easy read. I have spent many hours reading and contemplating it, and even now I continue to be surprised and delighted by the wisdom and insight that the book contains.

I believe that Kuhn's book is as revolutionary in its own way as Darwin's *On the Origin of Species*. Both authors seemed to know that their ideas would be difficult for the world to accept so they filled their books with numerous examples to illustrate and prove their point. What can make *The Structure of Scientific Revolutions* difficult to read, is that it assumes a background understanding about the history of science that many of us don't have. Even as a scientist I found myself needing to research some of the historical circumstances Kuhn discusses in order to grasp his point. In this chapter, I will do my best to outline his thesis before we go on to apply it to what quantum physics suggests about the nature of reality.

I want to start this exploration with an optimistic quotation from Benjamin Franklin, a leading scientist of his time, to an equally respected colleague Joseph Priestley.

> *The rapid Progress true Science now makes, occasions my Regretting sometimes that I was born so soon. It is impossible to imagine the Height to which may be carried in a 1000 Years the Power of Man over Matter. We may perhaps learn to deprive large Masses of their Gravity & give them absolute Levity, for the sake of easy Transport. Agriculture may diminish its Labour & double its Produce. All Diseases may by sure means be prevented or cured, not excepting even that of Old Age, and our Lives lengthened at pleasure even beyond the antediluvian Standard. (https://founders.archives.gov/documents/Franklin/01-31-02-0325)*

When this letter was written in 1780, science had already proven its profound potential to improve human life and was on its way to establishing its dominance over the way we think. This letter represents an important moment in history. It is a moment in which a new paradigm was born and established. It moved humanity out of the more superstitious assumptions of the medieval mind into the analytic powers of the modern mind. The world of the Middle Ages as viewed through modern eyes was brutal and largely incomprehensible. It was ruled by an all-knowing God who was generally hidden from view and communicated only through his advocates on earth. He was responsible for everything and demanded complete obedience. It was largely a terrifying world that left the individual with no ability to understand its workings.

As the so-called Age of Reason dawned, a process of enlightenment occurred in which people began to realize that the universe was actually governed by natural laws that could be observed, understood, and utilized for human advantage. The scientific method was developed as a way of hypothesizing about what laws were in operation, and then experimenting and testing to prove their validity and understand how to use them to improve the world. The universe was no longer incomprehensible, it was ordered by rules that could be observed, understood, and optimized for human benefit. The language that Franklin uses in his letter reflects the profoundly optimistic mood of science. The universe was not incomprehensible, it was understandable, and we were on the verge of understanding everything.

At least this is the story that science believed about itself. It is a story of a steady and unerring march to perfect knowledge about the universe and everything in it. It is a story that inevitably culminates in the perfect harmony of humanity with the natural laws of the universe. It is a story that has given us a sense of security in what otherwise might feel like a vast and dangerous universe. This is the story that Kuhn challenged in *The Structure of Scientific Revolutions*.

Kuhn's ideas are challenging because they expose the shortcomings of science, or at least the shortcomings of what science has largely become. The endeavor of science has undoubtedly led to vast improvements in human life, but that very success can mask its limitations and create a dangerous double-edged sword. If we look at our world, we see that the energy demands of accelerating technological growth has adversely shifted the delicate ecological balance of life on this planet. At the same time, our unconscious faith in science and the worldview that it has created, makes it all but impossible for us to even consider exploring other possibilities. In some ways, we have traded the unquestioned superstitious beliefs of the Middle Ages for a new set of equally unquestionable scientific assumptions about reality.

The root cause of the problem can be understood by examining the difference between science and scientism. You can think of scientism as a form of scientific fundamentalism. It is the view that the conclusions of science tell us the undisputed truth about reality. With the emergence of scientism, science becomes like a religion, and scientists like priests who are the ultimate authorities of what is true.

Of course, the assumption of scientism stands in

direct contrast with the true spirit of science, which is a fundamental assertion of the scientific method that no theory is ever ultimately proven to be true. All theories are considered provisional and will be continually tested through experimentation and either upheld or overthrown by a better theory. But that isn't necessarily how our society relates to science. Our culture is much more wrapped up in scientism than we might realize. An example that is common in advertising is the phrase 'scientifically proven,' which effectively means proven to be true.

The assumption that scientifically proven facts are always truer than any conclusions come to by any other means, is exactly what Kuhn was questioning. He wanted to open our eyes to the fact that the history of science is not a history of increasingly accurate accumulation of facts. We've been told a story about science. It's a story about how science leads to more and more true facts about nature. It is a story about the continual progress that science makes toward a complete understanding of the way things are. Kuhn makes clear that this story is not accurate. Science, in spite of its reputation, does not follow an unbroken path toward greater truth. The history of science zig zags back and forth between radically different conceptions of reality. The science of yesterday, did not directly lead to the science of today. And the science of tomorrow is not predictable from what we know today.

I want to share a story that was very illuminating for me. It happened while I was working as a junior member of the research and development team of the semiconductor laser company I mentioned earlier. That company, like so many others, had been founded by some brilliant MIT trained scientists and my job was to conduct experiments to test the theories that those senior scientists came up with.

One of the machines I operated was called a plasma etcher. It was a metal vacuum chamber that could pump down to almost complete vacuum. Once all of the air had been removed from it, you could deposit layers of metal that were only a few atoms thick. The whole operation was very delicate and had to be done in a cleanroom wearing gloves, gown, hat, and booties. At one point, we began having problems with the machine. It seemed that every time we ran it, copper would show up on everything. The copper was destroying our lasers. Fixing the plasma etcher became my only concern for the next few months. Every day we had a morning meeting where new theories were discussed, and new experiments and tests were devised for me to perform.

Often our daily meeting would go on for three hours as we all tried to figure out where this copper was coming from. Initially, we went through the obvious possibilities, impurities in the metal or in the semiconductor material itself. So, we would test those. When those didn't seem to be the source of the problem, we would have another theorizing session and another round of experiments. Over time pressure built up because we were losing money with every passing day and the theories got more and more extravagant. We started to wonder if the molecules in the semiconductor material were disintegrating and giving off electrons and protons that were recombining to form copper. We designed experiments to test that, then the next theory, and the next. Week after week, then a month, then two months, then three.

We didn't seem to be getting any closer to solving the problem. Everyone was getting frustrated. I, too, was getting frustrated and bored doing these tedious day long tasks, especially since I was gaining no knowledge from them and making no progress. One day, I decided I needed a few days off and I announced that I was going to clean the machine. We had already cleaned it a number of times, but this time I was going to really take it apart and give it a deep cleaning. Mainly, I wanted some time off, but it also seemed like a good idea since nothing else was working. I really did a good job, I kept pulling the machine apart and cleaning every piece individually.

At some point I happened to look under the stage where the metal sits and there I found the culprit. Wedged where it could hardly be seen, even with the machine pulled apart, there was a penny. Someone had dropped a penny in the machine. I don't know who, but that had been the problem all along. I put the machine back together and it worked just fine. I went to the senior scientists holding the penny. I told them that I had found the problem; there had been a penny in the machine. We ran some tests with the penny removed and there was no longer any copper on anything. Problem solved. Production went back up. Everybody was happy.

I had already read Thomas Kuhn's book when this happened, and for me the trouble around the penny perfectly illustrated his main point. Scientists believe that they are freely envisioning their theories when in fact the theories they can come up with are shaped by the assumptions they start with.

But let's move slowly. In the case of the hidden penny, our thinking was stuck in a rut, which is what Kuhn would speak about as being stuck in a paradigm. There were a lot of assumptions operating in the background of our theorizing that kept us from ever thinking about something as simple as the fact that maybe someone had dropped a penny in the machine. Once stuck in this rut, the brilliance of the scientists involved became a detriment because they knew enough and were clever enough to create an unending number of new theories about what was happening without exhausting the storehouse of ideas.

One of the central insights in *The Structure of Scientific Revolutions* is the realization that the theories that scientists devise are always being shaped by the presuppositions of the paradigm they're working in.

Each paradigm rests in a set of assumptions and all of the questions we can ask rest in the very same set of assumptions. Those assumptions are not just ideas we hold in our own minds, they exist in everyone else as well. They also lie hidden behind the words in every textbook we've ever read, and they are built into the functioning of all the scientific equipment we use. And as if that weren't already enough, they are also built into all the ways that we have learned to analyze experimental results and interpret data.

Our perception of reality is shaped by the assumptions of the current paradigm and those same assumptions limit the kinds of questions that we will ever think to ask. When we start looking for answers we do so using equipment that was built assuming the same basic ideas and no matter what we discover it will be interpreted through the very same set of assumptions. A paradigm is a circular loop from which there is rarely any escape. But, occasionally, a paradigm is broken, and a new paradigm is born.

In his book, Kuhn identifies three ways that paradigms get broken. One was exemplified by the situation I was in with the copper penny and the plasma etcher; namely, a persistent problem that cannot be solved in spite of our best efforts over a long period of time. Faced with the desperation caused by an unsolvable problem we might ask a radically different question or try something truly novel. Sometimes paradigms get broken this way.

The second way that paradigms are broken is when something is discovered that should not be possible. We will see later in this book that some of the results of quantum physics fall directly into this category. One of my intellectual heroes, the philosopher William James, felt that the existence of spiritual mystics and mediums presented the kind of anomalies that should make us question some of the most foundational assumptions of the modern scientific paradigm.

The third way that paradigms are sometimes broken happens when someone sees a radically different possibility through a leap of intuitive genius. If that person has the conviction not to back down from what they see, they may eventually convince others to see what they see. Einstein's famous paradigm-breaking theory of relativity is a great example of this.

As we said earlier, the story about science that we are told is that it grows by accumulating increasingly accurate knowledge about reality. Kuhn tells a very different story about the history of science. Yes, there are times when science does steadily increase our understanding of the world. During these times, scientists busy themselves expanding on what they already know. Kuhn calls this normal science.

Occasionally, during the course of normal scientific work, there arise persistent problems that can't be solved, or anomalies that can't be explained, or a brilliant leap of intuition that challenges the most fundamental assumptions of the scientific community.

Sometimes these disruptions lead to a period of revolutionary science and the birth of a new paradigm. During these remarkable times, scientists, or at least some of them, begin a critical examination of the rules by which science is being done. They are no longer just extending current theories. They are starting to question the validity of the theories themselves. When a new paradigm is established, science itself is changed. The science being done after a paradigm shift is not the same science that was being done before. The rules of science and the assumptions it works with are different. After a paradigm shift occurs, the world hasn't changed, but scientists live in a different world.

The paradigm that we live in is sometimes called the Cartesian/Newtonian worldview and it is based in the assumption of an objective reality. That means a reality that exists separate and apart from our experience of it. When this paradigm shift first emerged during the European Enlightenment, it created the space that allowed us to see the workings of nature more clearly. It led to the development of modern science and the many miraculous discoveries that science was subsequently able to make. Many of us recognize now that there are also some dramatic downsides to this paradigm. The distance that allowed us to see the world more clearly also seems to have led us dangerously close to the destruction of the planet we depend on for our very survival.

The work that I do is devoted to supporting the

emergence of a paradigm of unity and wholeness that can awaken new possibilities for the future of life on this planet. As I see it, this work involves both an inner experience of awakening to wholeness and a deep understanding of how our reality is shaped by the paradigm we live in. Evidence of a paradigm has been surfacing at the edges of human consciousness for a long time and the breakthroughs in physics that surfaced at the start of the twentieth century gave dramatic evidence that reality was very different than we had thought. In the remainder of this chapter, we will explore some of the remarkable ways that Thomas Kuhn encouraged us to question the nature of paradigms. In the following two chapters, we will start to explore the implications of quantum physics and how it points toward a new paradigm.

It is my assertion in writing this book that what Kuhn revealed about the nature of paradigm shifts in science applies to all of human life. We live inside a paradigm and the depth to which our experience is being shaped by that paradigm is more profound than we might imagine. The reality that we experience is inseparable from the paradigm through which we experience it.

So, what is the nature of a paradigm shift in which nothing changes, but everything's different?

Let's start our investigation by considering the possibility that there is no reality that is separate from our experience of it or our understanding about it.

That means that what is real and our perception of it are not two things, they are two aspects of the same thing. It means that our thoughts about what is real are part of reality itself.

Think about this, could you truly call something real if it could never be experienced by anyone or anything at any time? Can something that is utterly and completely incomprehensible and imperceptible be real? Another way to ask this question is to ask if things can have qualities independent of anyone's experience of them.

Imagine a bowl of soup. Is the soup bad or good, or does it become bad or good when someone tastes it? If one person thinks it's good and another person thinks it's bad, is the soup good or bad? In a simple case like this, most of us would agree that the soup isn't either bad or good. Those are qualities that occur in relation to the person eating it. And so, we would tend to say that the soup isn't good or bad except in the opinion of someone who tastes it.

The example of the quality of soup is simple, but what about the quality of existence. Does something exist in and of itself, or does it only come into existence when it is experienced by someone? Now this sounds nonsensical, but as we will see later in this book, this puzzling assertion is one of the implications of quantum physics. But let's not get too far ahead of ourselves, there is a lot more in *The Structure of*

Scientific Revolutions that we need to examine before we get too deep into the new physics.

We need to consider more deeply what role we play in the creation of reality. In the current paradigm, we are not taught that we play any part in the creation of reality. We are told that reality exists independent of us and then we discover things about it. But Kuhn's analysis of revolutionary leaps in the history of science made him question the current paradigm's assumption that reality is separate from our experience of it. Kuhn knew that traditionally science is seen as a way to accumulate facts about the world, but he started to question just what a fact is. In fact, what we consider to be the material world of facts may not be as factual as we think.

In some ways, Kuhn held a similar view of reality to that of William James. James described reality as being thick with layers of interpretation. We don't just experience reality, we interpret it. Something might independently exist underneath our perceptions, but our perceptions are always shaped by layers of assumption and interpretation.

I believe that the only useful way to talk about something called reality is to talk about it as an experienced reality. Any reality that cannot be experienced is essentially unreal. Of course, there might be a reality that we cannot experience, but that could be experienced at some other time, or in some other place by someone else, and that would be real. But a reality that cannot be experienced ever, anywhere, by anyone, is functionally unreal.

Kuhn brings this consideration to light in a powerful way by discussing the discovery of oxygen. In 1774, Joseph Priestley, the recipient of the letter from Ben Franklin that I quoted earlier, found that heating mercury oxide produced a gas. Priestley believed that the gas he discovered was a special kind of air. In 1778, Antoine Lavoisier duplicated Priestley's experimental results but identified the gas that was produced as the element oxygen. Kuhn raises the provocative question of which of the two actually discovered oxygen. Was it Priestley when he did the original experiment, or was it Lavoisier when he named the substance oxygen?

It is likely that we will naturally want to say Priestley should get the credit, but there is very good cause to question this. The situation reminds me of being a child and watching my little brother find something valuable on the ground without recognizing it for what it was and tossing it aside. Then, seeing me snatch it up he would exclaim, "Give that to me, I found it!" But did he? If you find something but don't recognize it for what it is, did you really find it?

What Joseph Priestley thought he discovered was air deprived of phlogiston. Phlogiston was believed to be a special substance that was the cause of burning. When anything burned, like mercury oxide, it was believed that it was because phlogiston was being removed. Lavoisier recognized that the gas that was created through Priestley's experiment was not dephlogisticated air, but a new element that he called oxygen. With this recognition, he opened the door that led to the development of modern chemistry, the periodic table of elements, and the understanding of how atoms combine to form compounds. The phlogiston theory was disproved and a new paradigm in science opened up.

Clearly, Lavoisier's recognition that the gas was oxygen was profoundly significant, but wasn't oxygen still oxygen even when Priestley thought it was dephlogisticated air?

Science textbooks would generally say yes, Joseph Priestley is usually recognized to be the person who discovered oxygen. This is partly because the current scientific paradigm believes that reality is what it is regardless of what we think about it. Oxygen was oxygen even when Priestley thought it was something else. It was oxygen even when people had no idea that it existed. Afterall, they were still breathing it every single day. It just seems like common sense, but the reason it feels that way is because in the current paradigm of scientific materialism reality is defined in terms of physical properties that are what they are regardless of what we think about them. Because the paradigm we live in tells us that matter is more primary than our ideas about it, Priestley obviously discovered oxygen, because oxygen was oxygen no matter what anyone thought about it.

Kuhn points out that this way of looking at science creates a story that helps us all feel secure. Reality is always there underneath all of our ideas about it. It never changes, and the history of science is the history of what we learn about a reality that never changes and will be always there. When science undergoes a revolutionary transition in any one of its fields it is reported on as if it were the inevitable outcome of what came before. The new paradigm was the next discovery about a reality. Kuhn wants us to question this. The world of science after the idea that everything we see is made up of the elements of the periodic table, was a completely different world than the one that still entertained the phlogiston theory. The phlogiston theory did not lead to our understanding of elements or to the recognition of oxygen.

Kuhn's point is that science is much more complicated than just a simple succession of discoveries about what is true, and reality is not just passively waiting to be discovered. Reality is being created as we develop ways to think about it. Maybe oxygen was not really discovered but invented. Maybe it would be better not to think of oxygen as just the name of a material substance, but as a way of thinking about a material substance. The way we think about that substance unleashes certain potentials into reality, and in this case, the creation of the periodic table of elements and modern chemistry. At the same time, the way we think also hides other possibilities from view, like Priestley's belief in the phlogiston theory hid the idea of elements.

Our current paradigm which sees reality as fundamentally material, naturally recognizes Joseph Priestley as the person who discovered oxygen. The question I want us to consider is, could there be a different conception of what is real that would include our observation of reality as part of what creates reality and, in that world, would we be more inclined to say that oxygen wasn't discovered until Lavoisier recognized it as oxygen?

What if reality was not defined by physical properties but by living potentials? Oxygen therefore would not be defined by its physical properties, but by what it made possible. Lavoisier's naming of oxygen and his recognition of it as an element, made a lot of things possible that wouldn't have been possible otherwise. In a world where reality was defined by possibility rather than physicality, Lavoisier might be recognized as having made the more significant discovery. It wasn't just the discovery of oxygen, but the naming of it, that unleashed the potentials of modern chemistry.

Some of those reading this book might at this point start to object that I am defining reality in human terms, and according to our current paradigm that is bad, reality is supposed to be objectively real. Reality is supposed to exist independent of our human experience of it.

The premise of this little book is that there is a

way in which reality might not exist independent of our experience of it. There might not be any reality that is just sitting there waiting to be discovered. Perhaps reality is being created in each and every moment, as it is being experienced. This is not the way we have been trained to think, but it is the direction that the discoveries of quantum physics point us. Please bear with me just a little longer before we get to those extraordinary discoveries. We are not quite done setting the philosophical ground for our exploration of quantum physics.

We can further illustrate the point we are making by introducing the philosophy of Martin Heidegger and discussing a film called *The Gods Must Be Crazy*.

When we start to consider that reality could be defined by possibility, we are entering terrain that was explored by the German philosopher Martin Heidegger. In this way of seeing, oxygen was not oxygen until Lavoisier named it, because that is when the possibilities of being oxygen became available. This brings us to one of the ideas that was developed by Heidegger.

Heidegger believed that for thousands of years, human beings had misidentified the nature of what it means 'to be'. From the time of the great Greek thinkers, the fundamental nature of 'being' was thought to be substance. All of reality was made up of substances. In other words, we live in a universe made of 'stuff' of one kind or another. Heidegger in his philosophy corrects this. He recognizes that one level of being is rooted in substance, but another equally real level of being is based on utility.

The mode of being that is based on utility has to do with the usefulness of things. It is the mode of being a tool or equipment, Heidegger's famous example is a hammer. As a substance, a hammer is a piece of wood with a heavy metal end. The substance of the hammer has intrinsic properties. It is heavy, it is smooth, etc. But those intrinsic characteristics do not make it a hammer. This object only becomes a hammer when it is recognized to be a hammer by someone who knows what it is and how to use it. The characteristics of being a hammer are not intrinsic to the hammer – they are interdependent with the person who would use it, and the world in which it would be used. A hammer is just a piece of wood and metal until it appears in a world where it can be used among people who know how to use it... Then, it becomes a hammer.

This second mode of being is humorously illustrated in the film *The Gods Must Be Crazy*. In the film, a small plane flies over a jungle and the pilot throws an empty Coke bottle out the window and it lands on the ground near a village of native peoples.

One of the native people finds the Coke bottle and brings it back to the village where nobody's ever seen a Coke bottle or anything like it before. The movie unfolds as the native people attempt to figure out what this gift from the gods is for. The central question that the film asks is, is a Coke bottle still a Coke bottle if nobody knows what it is?

The glass that the bottle is made of is a substance that continues to exist even if no one knows what a Coke bottle is. But the function of a Coke bottle, the possibility of using it to store Coke in, only exists when someone recognizes it. The recognition of its function is what makes a Coke bottle a Coke bottle and not just a piece of glass. This bottle is not just an object in the physical universe, it is also a tool in the world of people who might use it. The physical universe is one level of reality and the world of meaningful and useful things is another, and both are equally real.

When Thomas Kuhn makes the point that when a paradigm shifts nothing changes, but everything's different, he is essentially speaking about these two levels of being. The physical world of the universe does not change, but the meaningful world of utility changes dramatically. The naming of oxygen did not change the physical world, but it dramatically altered the meaningful world and created a new set of possibilities. In one sense, the world did not change at all, but in another sense, we live in a new world.

So far, this probably all makes sense to you. We all know for instance that the printed paper in our pocket is not legal tender unless it is recognized as such by the people around us. But our exploration has only just begun, and we will continue by using some of the dramatic discoveries of quantum physics to see just how far down the co-creative nature of reality actually goes. When and where does the meaningful world of subjectivity end, and the physical universe of objective facts begin?

If you are not completely confused by quantum mechanics, you do not understand it.

- JOHN WHEELER

02

Do Time and Space Exist?

"Science cannot solve the ultimate mystery of nature. And that is because, in the last analysis, we ourselves are a part of the mystery that we are trying to solve."

-MAX PLANK

Now we are going to take our exploration further by looking at the implications of quantum physics, but before we get to quantum theory, it will be good to start with some good old-fashioned classical physics.

If you stand on a highway, say out in a flat desert, and a motorcycle speeds by, you will notice something. As the motorcycle approaches you, the sound of its engine is high pitched, but as soon as it passes, the sound drops to a lower pitch. Why does this happen? Sound is a wave, which means it is not really a tangible object, it is just energy that passes as waves through the air. When the motorcycle speeds towards you, the crest of each wave of sound is closer to the last one because the motorcycle is moving in the same direction that the sound waves are traveling. The waves are getting crunched. When the motorcycle passes you, the crest of each wave becomes further apart because the motorcycle is moving away from you and spreading the waves out. So, in front of the motorcycle the waves get crunched more closely together and behind it they spread further apart from each other. This is known as the Doppler Effect.

The effect illustrates the wave nature of sound. We hear sound because the denser air of the crest of a sound wave hits our eardrum and pushes it inward, and the less dense trough pulls it back out. When sound waves are packed more tightly together the eardrum moves in and out faster. That gives the sound a high pitch. When the waves are spread further apart, the eardrum moves more slowly and that creates a low pitch. If you take away all the air in the room, you will hear no sound at all. Sound is not an object, it only exists as waves in air. Air is the medium, the waves that travel through the air move your eardrum. We call those waves sound waves, but without the air there is no sound.

The same thing is also true of water waves. If you stand on a beach you can see the waves rolling in, but would there still be a wave if all the water were gone? Of course not. A wave is not a thing that can be separated from the water. A wave is an energetic configuration of water. As we move into our discussion of quantum theory, it will be important that we understand that the word 'wave' is used to describe energy traveling through a medium like air or water. A wave does not exist physically separate from the air or the water.

Up until the advent of quantum theory, light was also believed to be an energy wave because light has wave-like properties. Just like sound, light can change frequency. The warmer colors of light like red, yellow, and orange, have lower frequencies. The cooler colors, purple, blue, and green, have higher frequencies. Also, light, like sound, bends around corners. Sunlight shining through a window will light up the whole room, just like you would be able to hear someone talking loudly outside throughout the whole house. Waves bend around corners.

Light has long been known to have wave-like properties, which raises the question, what is the medium that light travels through? Sound travels through air, but what does light travel through? For a long time, many people hypothesized the existence of a substance called aether. It was believed that there was an air like substance that light must travel through because it is impossible to have a wave without a medium. This was the state of affairs in physics leading up to the twentieth century, but then things started to get strange, because it was then that the quantum nature of light was discovered.

Any wave can get smaller and smaller until it disappears all together. What they discovered with light is that it can get dimmer and dimmer and dimmer, but at some point, it can't get any dimmer. There is a limit to how dim light can get before it disappears and that limit is a very discrete number, a specific quantity. No matter how hard you try you can never produce light with less energy than that minimum amount.

Now this was strange because light was thought to be a wave, but it was acting more like a particle. Imagine that there is a wave of tennis balls passing through the air over your head. There are hundreds of them. You take more and more of them away, and as you do this, the wave of tennis balls gets smaller and smaller. But at some point, there is only one tennis ball left. You can't have any less than that. Light seemed to be operating in the same way and scientists started to imagine that light was made up of light particles called photons that traveled like waves of tennis balls through the air. This meant that light didn't need a medium. Light was a thing!

Imagine an ocean wave that is discovered to actually be made up of little, tiny ocean waves, millions of them. These are the ocean wave particles. Maybe they were the size of peas and you could hold one in your hand. Of course, if you think about an ocean wave it doesn't make sense. An ocean wave isn't a collection of little things, it is an energized configuration of water. It is a wave. The idea of teeny tiny ocean waves that can exist independent of water and combine to form a big wave is absurd. Well, the idea that light would be made of particles was equally absurd when it was discovered. Waves should not be divisible into tiny waves.

It was actually Albert Einstein that proposed that light is not a wave that propagates through space, but a discrete wave packet that can act like a particle rather than a wave. He came to these conclusions based on something called the photoelectric effect and he called the individual particles of light, photons.

Up until the discovery of the photoelectric effect, light was considered to be an energy wave traveling through a mysterious medium that was yet to be discovered. The transition that occurred in physics around this discovery would be something like discovering that sound was created out of little specks of dust that screamed in your ear. In order to imagine a particle of light, scientists had to adjust their entire view of what light was. They had to enter into a new paradigm when it came to their understanding of light. This was not an easy transition, and not every scientist made it.

This book is about the spiritual implications of quantum physics, but I am going to avoid making any claims about what reality must be like because of quantum physics. I don't know what the world must be like. To me, the big implication of quantum physics is that the paradigm we live in, our fundamental understanding of reality, needs to change. When the early physicists started to encounter the bizarre findings of this new science, they knew that things had to change. This was a revolution in science. It was a revolution in our understanding of reality. It was a paradigm shift.

Paradigm shifts like this are very difficult to make because they don't just challenge what we think about reality, they challenge our experience of reality. This is very important to understand. The paradigm shift that quantum physics points to challenges our actual experience of reality. That is why I see those implications as spiritual in nature. They don't just challenge us cognitively or emotionally; they challenge us experientially.

I will briefly use an example that I have written about many times to illustrate what I mean. It is about a teacher who asks a student why it was that for so long people believed that the sun went around the earth, even though it was always the earth that was rotating. The student answers by saying that it must be because it looks like the sun is going around the earth. The teacher counters by asking what it would look like if the earth were rotating.

It is a simple story, but it illustrates a very profound point. We can all relate to the fact that it looks like the sun is going around the earth, but of course it would look exactly the same way if the earth were rotating – because the earth *is* rotating! What this shows is how profoundly our perception of reality is conditioned by the way we think about reality. If we think that the sun is moving around the earth, then it will look to us as if that were the case. If we talk about the sun rising in the morning, it will look like the sun is rising, when in reality, it isn't. It looks like the sun is rising because we think it is. Our perception of reality conforms to what we believe.

For instance, if we started to talk about the appearance of the sun in the morning in terms of the rotation of the earth by calling it 'morning rotation' rather than 'sunrise', our perception would shift. We would eventually start to feel the earth rotating forward as the sun became more visible in the sky. Our new belief would alter our perception so that it would feel like the earth were rotating. At that point any school child would tell you that it just feels like the earth is rotating. Nothing would have changed, but everyone would live in a different world!

The relationship between what we think about reality and how we experience reality is what makes paradigm shifting so difficult. In so many ways how we think about reality and how we speak about it, are constantly reinforcing a perception of reality that matches what we believe to be true. It is very difficult for us to experience a reality that is fundamentally at odds with what we believe to be true. The internal language we use when we think and the external language that we share with others, create and solidify our experience of reality. Changing the way we think and talk can have a dramatic effect over what we see and feel.

In the first chapter, we spoke about how part of the essence of the scientific method is the understanding that all theories are just theories and can never be proven to be true. They must continually be tested, and we must always remain open to the possibility that any theory might be proven false the next time it is tested. This attitude is meant to generate the open-mindedness that science aspires to, but it also lands us in a perplexing philosophical problem, the problem of verisimilitude.

Verisimilitude is an ancient word which essentially means the feeling of being true. Some statements feel truer than others. This is a problem, because feeling true, doesn't necessarily mean being true. The fact that it feels like the sun is going around the earth, doesn't mean that it is. Our perception of reality is shaped by what we believe in the first place, and once our perception is shaped, it is very difficult to imagine reality any other way. This is why the philosopher Alfred North Whitehead said that it takes a very unusual mind to undertake an analysis of the obvious.

So, the problem with verisimilitude is that what feels obviously true to us, becomes almost impossible to question. This becomes particularly challenging if we don't already know what is actually true. It is easy to recognize the difference between a statement that is true and another one that is not. For instance, it's easy to see that the statement, I am a human being, is a true statement, and the statement, I am a goat, is a false statement. Very simple because we already know what a human is and what a goat is. One statement is true and the other is false. The problem of verisimilitude arises when we try to determine which of two false statements is closer to the truth than the other. For instance, is the statement, I am a goat, truer than the statement, I am an elephant? On what grounds would we determine the relative truth of two false statements? Am I closer to being a goat than I am to being an elephant when in fact I am neither?

If all scientific theories are considered to be provisional and perpetually unproven, then how can we possibly determine which unproven theory is closer to the truth than the other when we don't know what the truth is. It's like driving your car without knowing where you're going and trying to figure out which road to take to get there.

The results that came out of the early quantum experiments challenged our conception of time and space so dramatically that it was hard to know what they implied. Even some of the greatest scientists had a hard time embracing the bizarre world of quantum physics. Einstein himself, one of the central architects of this revolution, even found some of its more radical implications impossible to accept.

The fundamental view of reality that most of us hold is a few hundred years old. It is a vision of a universe that extends infinitely in three dimensions of space and progresses through a linear process of time. This understanding of space and time proves to be very valuable for most of our daily activities, like driving to the store or placing things on a shelf, but once we start to look at the subatomic world, it doesn't hold up anymore.

The challenge that the new physics presents is that it reveals a world that runs counter to our current perception of reality. We simply cannot understand this new world and hold on to our current understanding of reality at the same time. The two are incompatible with each other.

One of the most famous early experiments of the new physics was the double slit experiment, which illustrates the bizarre implications of the dual, wave and particle, nature of light.

The set up for the double slit experiment is easy to picture. It is basically a surface with two parallel slits cut into it that light can shine through. Before we start talking about light, let's think for a minute about water. Imagine a breakwater on the shore with two openings in it. As the waves pass through the openings, they will spread on the other side in circles that expand in all directions. That's because, as we said before, waves bend around corners. The waves that emerge through one of the openings will eventually start running into waves that passed through the other.

The same will be true of light waves passing through the two slits. The light spreads out in concentric circles and the light from one slit will eventually make contact with the light from the other one. Now we add a screen to our experimental set up so that the light hits it. Because the waves of light from one slit overlap with the light from the other, they produce what is an interference pattern on the screen. The place where the light crest of a wave from one slit overlaps the crest of a light wave from the other shows up brightly on the screen in that spot, any place where the troughs of two light waves meet will cancel out leaving no light in that spot.

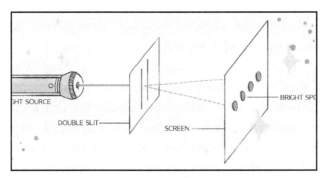

Figure 1. The Double Slit Experiment

Now let's not think about light or water waves, but bullets instead. Imagine that there are two slits in a castle wall, and you were shooting bullets through them. Bullets fly straight, they don't bend around corners like waves do. So, if there were people inside, they could hide around the corner and not get shot. It also means that all the bullets will land on the wall roughly opposite whichever slit they entered through. Bullet holes will accumulate in just two places on the opposite wall. No matter how many bullets you shoot they will all hit the wall opposite in one of the two places. No bullets will bend around the corner of one slit and interfere with the bullets passing through the other one. Bullets travel in straight lines. They always stay in their own lane.

We don't expect to see just two light spots when we shine light through two slits. We expect an interference pattern of many bright spots because waves travel around corners and interfere with each other. And ordinarily, when we shine light through two slits, that is exactly what we see.

Then scientists wondered about something. What if they only allowed one photon at a time to pass through the slits? When they tried, they still found an interference pattern. Now this was weird. How did one photon interfere with itself? A single photon must either pass through one slit or the other. If you shoot photons through a surface with only one slit you don't get an interference pattern, but add a second slit and you do, even though any one photon only passes through one slit. How did it know the other slit was there?

To get a better idea of what was happening, scientists put a detector on one of the slits so they would know which slit the photon traveled through to reach the screen.

Now that they knew which slit each photon traveled through, something really weird happened. The interference pattern was gone and now there were just two spots of light on the screen. The photons were acting like bullets, not waves.

When the scientists didn't know which slit the photon went through the light acted like a wave, when they did know, it acted like a particle. Without

THE SPIRITUAL IMPLICATIONS OF QUANTUM PHYSICS

knowing, wave, with knowing, particle. How did the particle know that the scientists knew? How does what a scientist know affect how reality shows up? This was really weird.

This experiment opens up some very interesting questions about the relationship between what we know, and what reality is. It appears that our experience of reality actually affects reality! We are not separate from reality observing it from a distance. Our observations are shaping reality. This is a truly unexpected result, and we haven't caught up with it nearly a century later.

Another remarkable discovery of quantum physics is known as quantum entanglement. To describe the phenomenon briefly, imagine that two electrons are created in the same place at the same time. One of the properties of an electron is spin and you can only have two electrons in the same place if they have opposite spin, one has a negative spin and the other has a positive spin.

What you find is that if two electrons are created together with opposite spin and you shoot them out to opposite ends of the universe and then change the spin of one of them, the spin of the other will change at the same time. Even though they are no longer together, each one shifts immediately in response to a shift in the other, and by immediately, I mean at exactly the same time, no matter how far apart they are.

Let's imagine that there are two basketballs sitting

on the floor on opposite sides of a gymnasium. Now imagine that you pick one of them up and as you do, you see that the one seventy-five feet away move upward exactly in unison with the ball in your hands. So, you start bouncing the ball in your hand and you see the one on the other side of the room bouncing exactly in unison. How bizarre is this? Can you imagine how mind-blown you would be if this happened to you? That is how the first scientists who discovered quantum entanglement must have felt.

Imagine that I was demonstrating this to you in a room right now. I was moving the basketball on one side of the room and the one on the other side moved in unison. You would assume it must be a trick. You would inspect for mirrors, some kind of remote-control motor, string, etc. You would have to assume that there was a trick, because what you are seeing is impossible. But why do we think it is impossible? Only because we haven't seen anything like it before. If we see something that has never been seen before, we feel compelled to assume that it's impossible.

Even the brilliant Albert Einstein dismissed quantum entanglement calling it spooky action at a distance. If I could show it to you with basketballs you would be inclined to believe it because, as the saying goes, seeing is believing. But these experimental results of quantum physics have proven reliable for decades and they have hardly even begun to touch our popular conceptions of time, space, and consciousness.

THE SPIRITUAL IMPLICATIONS OF QUANTUM PHYSICS

The inexplicable results of the double slit experiment and quantum entanglement call into question our most basic assumptions about time, space, and consciousness. According to our current view of reality, light should not be able to know that a second slit is present, or that it has been seen by a pair of eyes. Just like an electron on one side of the galaxy should not be able to know that the spin of its sister particle has changed.

Remember that one of Thomas Kuhn's reasons that paradigm shifts occur is because discoveries are made that should not be possible. Nearly 100 years ago, discoveries began being made in the domain of physics that should simply not be possible. These discoveries fundamentally call into question our basic notions of time, space, and consciousness.

As we bring this part of our discussion to a close, I want you to consider the possibility that time and space do not exist. Maybe time and space are properties of things, not properties of space.

We can only measure things. We can't measure space. Even if you bring a ruler into space you are not really measuring space, you are measuring the length of the ruler, which is a thing. When we measure something, we assume we are measuring the space that it takes up, but what if we are not? We assume that if we remove the thing from its location that the space remains, what if it doesn't?

What if things create space rather than take up

space? I realize that this doesn't make much sense, but as we have already explained, it can't make sense because the paradigm that we live in doesn't allow it to make sense. One possible implication of quantum physics is nonlocality, which means that everything exists in the same place because there is no space. Everything is just here.

The universe that quantum physics reveals defies our understanding of time implying that time may not exist in anything like the way we have been taught to assume. The current paradigm presents us with an expanse of three-dimensional space filled with things that move through time. Quantum physics presents us with things affecting one another instantaneously over vast distances. Information seems to travel from one place to another without needing any time to do it in. Our common understanding of time and space must change dramatically to accommodate this.

We are taught that time is always moving forward, but maybe quantum physics is telling us that there is no time at all. Afterall, when we measure time, we are actually measuring movement which leads us to imagine we are measuring time.

Let's think about it. Let's say you want to measure how long it takes you to read this book. You look at your clock and record the time when you start. The minute hand and the hour hand of the clock move until you are done reading. You then look at the time again. Let's say it took three hours. You didn't really

THE SPIRITUAL IMPLICATIONS OF QUANTUM PHYSICS

measure time, you measured how far the hands on the clock moved. (If we had a digital watch instead of a clock with hands, the same idea would apply, but it would be less easy to visualize the movement that was being measured.)

The point here is not to try to concoct new concepts of time and space, it is simply to realize that we have very strong ideas about time and space that are going to need to be creatively challenged in order to embrace the implications of quantum science. And the same goes for consciousness. How can a photon know if another slit exists, and how can it know that it is being detected? How can the fact that we know where a photon is, affect how it behaves? How can an electron on one side of the galaxy know what its sister is doing on the other? Our entire concept of what it means to know and who it is that knows is ripe for questioning.

A book called *The Quantum Labyrinth* tells the story of two physicists who had the kind of creative imagination that quantum results require. I will tell you just one of the ideas they arrived at to illustrate the point. It is called the one-electron postulate.

As the story is relayed in the book, a young and brilliant graduate student named Richard Feynman answered his telephone late one night to find that his equally brilliant thesis advisor, Professor John Wheeler, was calling unexpectedly. Wheeler was very excited because he claimed that he had figured out why every electron ever discovered has exactly the same qualities.

There is only one electron in the universe!

You see, Wheeler believed that a positron, which is a particle identical to an electron but with a positive rather than a negative charge, is really just an electron that is moving backward in time. So, there could be just one electron moving all over the universe forward and backward in time, giving it the potential to be everywhere at once. If it moves from New York to Paris in an instant, then moves backward in time to Mexico City, then forward to New Delhi, then backwards again to Tokyo, no time will pass because each back-and-forth trip will cancel out. Potentially, the electron can be everywhere in the universe at the same moment. Wheeler had figured it out. There is only one electron in the universe!

I wouldn't get too busy trying to figure out if this is true or not, it is possible and that is enough to make the point. The real value of this story is that it gives all of us permission to liberate our minds to be wildly creative. Afterall, if two internationally acclaimed scientists are allowed to imagine that the entire universe might contain only one time-traveling electron, what's limiting our imaginations?

My reason for writing this book is because I believe that the amount of change that our world needs right now will demand an enormous amount of open-minded imagination. It won't come from creeping out slowly beyond the edges of what we already know. We need to entertain radically different possibilities, which is what paradigm shifters have done throughout history.

> *In the beginning there were only probabilities. The universe could only come into existence if someone observed it. It does not matter that the observers turned up several billion years later.*
>
> – MARTIN REES

03

Has Consciousness Evolved?

"Not only does God play dice but he sometimes throws them where they cannot be seen."

– STEPHEN HAWKING

JEFF CARREIRA

In this final chapter we will turn our attention directly onto the question of consciousness and we will start by outlining in brief how it is currently believed that consciousness evolved on this planet in the first place.

The dominant story about evolution in the scientific paradigm tells us that the universe started with a big bang. Of course, the obvious question that raises is, what was there before the big bang? The answer is nothing. Before the Big Bang there was no time, no space, no energy, no things – nothing. The explosion of the Big Bang was an explosion of time, space, energy, and material particles. The Big Bang didn't happen at any point in time. It didn't happen in space. It happened before time and space existed.

The Big Bang Theory, as it is known, is not a very good theory for more reasons than we will go into here, but I can tell you that I did spend time reading literature both pro and con and I came to the conclusion that it isn't sound. There just isn't a better theory out there yet. To me, and obviously people differ on this, saying the universe was created in a big bang is no more explanatory than saying it was created by God. The Big Bang seems like a scientifically comfortable way of saying God.

But I digress, I really just want to outline the story of evolution as it is generally told.

There was a big bang and out of that explosion time, space, matter, and energy emerged. This was followed by an unimaginably long period of time, billions of years, when the universal soup mixed together. Atoms combined to form the elements of the periodic table and eventually stars and planets formed. Then on at least one planet, ours, something very interesting happened. Something became alive.

No one knows where it was that life first appeared on Earth or how, but it must have, because there is life here now. Once life emerged, it evolved through a process of natural selection until eventually some living thing could perceive its surroundings and respond to what it perceived. It became conscious. Again, no one knows how life became conscious, but it must have, because we are conscious now.

In short, the universe started with an explosion of dead, unconscious matter that evolved over time to become alive and conscious.

If you have not seen the animated short called *Appling* created by Matt Stone and Trey Parker, I highly recommend it. This brief two-minute animation was created from an audio clip of a teaching by the great Western teacher of Buddhism, Alan Watts.

The cartoon begins showing apples growing on a tree and saying that the tree is doing something intelligent; it is 'appling'. It goes on to describe a group of aliens who discover a dead planet and dismiss it as nothing but a bunch of rocks. The aliens return millions of years later and find the dead planet is now full of people. They were wrong. The planet wasn't dead, it was alive and intelligent. It did something smart, it peopled. Watts sums up the point this way, "We grow out of this world, in exactly the same way that the apples grow on the apple tree. If evolution means anything, it means that."

I want you to consider the possibility that consciousness didn't evolve on this planet; it was here from the start.

Among spiritual groups, it's hard to find anyone who would self-identify as a materialist, but most of us are much more materialistic than we realize. I don't mean that we like to have nice things, I mean we assume without realizing it that matter, things we can see and touch, are more real than the things we can only feel and think about in our minds.

In philosophy, the opposite of materialism is an idealism. A materialist believes that the foundation of reality is matter and an idealist believes that the foundation of reality is consciousness. The story of evolution that I recounted above is a materialistic interpretation of evolution. It starts with matter and adds consciousness later. It is a story of evolution in which matter is seen as primary and consciousness as a secondary byproduct of matter.

When I say that we are more materialistic than we realize, I am talking about a very basic attitude toward what is real. When I pick up a glass from the table, I assume that I am picking up a thing called a glass. I assume it is made of atoms in a very particular arrangement. I assume that the glass in my hand is a real material thing that exists independent of me and my experience of it. That is a materialistic attitude.

An idealist would see it differently. They would see that they were having an experience of picking up a glass. They would not assume that the glass was real outside of the experience of it. In other words, reality to an idealist is more like a dream. In a dream you might pick up a glass and it feels real, but when you wake up in the morning you realize that it was only a dream. The glass was not real outside of the dream. In an analogous way, the idealist, does not see the material world as something that exists outside of our experience of it.

We are all trained materialists and so we assume that the world contains real material things that have characteristics and qualities that belong to them. The things in the world are not just real in our experience, they are real independently whether we experience them or not. This is the dominant way of thinking in

THE SPIRITUAL IMPLICATIONS OF QUANTUM PHYSICS

our culture and the language we use keeps reinforcing that reality in the same way that using the word 'sunrise' keeps reinforcing the experience of the sun going around the earth.

I've had very profound spiritual experiences that have left me convinced that my experience of reality, at least as far as I can be certain of, is only an experience of reality. I can't be sure that there is anything physically real underneath it. Of course, in my day-to-day life when I pick up a glass, I talk about it as if it were a real thing that exists outside of my experience of it. We live in a culture that is very deeply steeped in materialism, and our perception of reality is dramatically shaped by materialistic assumptions. So, we perceive a universe of three-dimensional space filled with things that change over time. The reason why the implications of quantum physics have proven so difficult for our culture to assimilate is because they directly contradict the way we have been trained to perceive reality.

In this chapter we will continue to question our materialistic assumptions about reality and the linguistic conditioning that turns those assumptions into our perceived reality. It is interesting to note that the materialistic worldview that we currently live in is a relative newcomer to the world. Up until the European Enlightenment a few hundred years ago, most human beings had been idealists throughout the rest of human history. I want to be clear that there is no definitive proof that the materialist perception of reality is wrong, but there's also no definitive proof that it's right either. It's the paradigm we were born into, so it feels right, but that doesn't make it so.

The basic questions we will address in this chapter are, what is consciousness? and how did it emerge out of unconscious matter? In 1991, Daniel Dennett, a philosopher at Tufts University, published a book called *Consciousness Explained*. I had a few opportunities to meet with Dennett in his office at the university and he was generous enough to discuss his idea of consciousness with me. I don't entirely remember the content of our discussions, but I know in a general sense that Dennett believed discussions of subjectivity were unscientific. Some of his detractors suggested that his book might better have been called 'Consciousness Ignored'.

The Australian philosopher David Chalmers spoke about The Hard Problem of Consciousness, which he contrasted with the easy problems. The easy problems are essentially questions about how the brain functions and how cognition happens. The hard problem of consciousness is the problem of what consciousness is in the first place. Chalmers claimed that Dennett had skipped the hard problem entirely.

We can illustrate the hard problem by asking ourselves how it is that we think. The easy problem is about what happens in the brain while we are thinking. The hard problem is how all that brain activity leads to the experience of thinking. How does thinking happen? Do you really know how you think? Is thinking an activity that you do, or is it something that just happens?

This question extends to the question of how we know anything at all. Right now, we are all having a subjective experience of reality. I see the world around me, it feels like something to be in a body. If I pick up a glass of water, I know that it is water and I know what it will taste like if I drink it. How does any of that happen?

If we stick with the easy problem, we will explain it all in terms of electrical impulses that take place in the brain. But that doesn't solve the hard problem. The hard problem is figuring out how those electrical impulses give rise to our subjective experience of feeling, thinking, and knowing.

Going back to the story of evolution we start with the assumption that this planet was initially a pile of unconscious rock that didn't have any experience at all. Later, something started to move and respond to the things around it; it was now alive. And eventually, some living thing started to have an inner subjective experience of reality; and it was now conscious. How did this happen?

In his theory of Biocentrism, scientist and philosopher Robert Lanza points out that in order to accept our current view of evolution we have to be comfortable with the fact that we have no idea how life or consciousness appeared in the universe. This seems like two massive omissions in the theory. In the books *Biocentrism* and *Beyond Biocentrism*, written with Bob Berman, Lanza uses his scientific background to argue that if we assume that the universe was alive and conscious from the very start, we wouldn't have to explain how consciousness and life appeared in it.

He argues that the results of quantum physics already show us that at an atomic level something like consciousness already exists. Photons seem to be conscious of two slits and aware that they have been seen passing through one of them, and particles seem to be aware of the spin of their sister. Perhaps we don't live in an unconscious universe in which some conscious living things eventually appeared. Perhaps the universe is itself conscious. Maybe everything in the universe is consciousness. Not just humans and animals, but bacteria, flowers, rocks, and even space. Maybe, it's somehow all conscious.

In our current materialistic paradigm this seems absurd. It isn't something we can prove with certainty, so it's probably not worth putting a lot of time into thinking about it. What does it even mean that a rock is conscious? It is absurd even to consider that.

It is important, however, to think about why it seems so ludicrous to consider the possibility of a conscious universe. The idea that the entire universe is conscious is so difficult to imagine because our idea of what it means to be conscious is wedded to our own experience of consciousness. We assume that to be conscious means to be conscious the way humans are conscious.

There has been a great deal of excitement over the past few decades about the possibility of artificial intelligence. There is even a test developed by the computer science pioneer, Alan Turing, to determine the existence of artificial intelligence. Essentially the test, called a Turning Test, involves asking a computer questions and listening to its answers. If a human being asking the questions cannot tell if the answers are coming from a machine or a human, then we have to assume the computer is intelligent – at least as intelligent as we are.

The Turning Test was brought to the big screen in the science fiction movie Blade Runner. Rick Deckard, the main character in the story, uses Turning Tests to identify androids that are posing as humans. In a particularly dramatic scene, he speaks with someone who looks perfectly human, but as his questions become less literal and more metaphorical the computer brain of the android can no longer answer. Deckard knows he is dealing with a machine, not an intelligent human lifeform.

What this scene illustrates is very profound. We equate intelligence, and its sister, consciousness, with human intelligence and human consciousness. We define consciousness in relationship to our experience of it, then we look at the universe and it appears that we are the only things that are conscious. This anthropocentric conception of consciousness leaves us closed off to other forms of consciousness that might exist all around us. Because of the way we understand consciousness, we tend to imagine that something is conscious if it appears to exhibit the kind of consciousness that we have. Of course, this is changing. Some of us recognize the consciousness of animals, and even plants, but we have a long way to go before rocks would commonly be considered conscious.

Some years ago, I watched a debate between four very well-known public intellectuals. Three of them were philosophers who had a firm materialist bias. The other was a medical doctor and well-known spiritual writer who was defending the view that the universe is conscious.

The debate became a bit of a three against one intellectual smackdown. The medical doctor was someone I knew and respected, but in this debate, he was fighting a losing battle. Essentially, the doctor kept explaining and describing his belief in an idealistic view of a conscious universe. He spoke passionately and eloquently, but no matter what he said one of the other three would respond by demanding that the doctor prove his claims.

I found it painful to watch. The doctor seemed to take the bait every time. He would restate his claim about the universe being conscious becoming more and more frustrated that the other debaters would not engage with the idea beyond demanding proof. I kept wanting him to switch the conversation around. I wanted him to ask the others to prove that matter exists, or time, or space.

If he had asked, they would not have been able to prove these claims either, except maybe to say that their existence is obvious. This brings us again to the challenge of verisimilitude – some things just seem true to us. But things that appear to be true aren't necessarily truer. It once felt obvious that the earth was flat, but that didn't make it true. If you look out over the horizon, it looks like the earth is flat, but that doesn't mean it is. If you touch a table it feels like a perfectly solid object, but science would tell us that every seemingly solid object is almost entirely composed of empty space, with only a tiny number of solid particles floating around in it. The fact that it feels entirely solid, doesn't mean that it is.

The dominant paradigm doesn't feel obliged to prove itself, even though it feels justified in demanding that any alternative view must. The fact is, the currently dominant paradigm of scientific materialism has plenty of obvious shortcomings. It can't explain the origins of the universe, and it can't explain the emergence of life or consciousness. These might simply be things that aren't understood yet and will be later, or they may be evidence that the entire paradigm needs to be replaced by something else.

I saw Robert Lanza speak at a conference once and

his passion for a paradigm shift impressed me a great deal. What I heard then, and later read in his books, is that he believes that the current paradigm keeps us locked in a classical perception of reality that is a few hundred years old. We are experiencing the world the way that classical physics envisioned it – a vast expanse of empty space filled with solid objects. We experience the world that way because we have been trained to, and because we do, that reality feels true to us.

As I said earlier, even the great Albert Einstein never got fully on board with quantum mechanics because he was committed to some of the principles of classical physics and wasn't ready or willing to give them up. Eventually he fell out of step with a scientific revolution that he himself had helped initiate. Of course, let's not sell Einstein short. His theory of relativity dramatically changed our notions of time and space, which Einstein concluded were nothing but stubborn habits of perception.

The physics of relativity theory and quantum mechanics have dramatically changed our understanding of reality, but now a century later, most of us still live in a classical world. A big part of why we all find it difficult to get on board with the reality implied by quantum physics is because reality just doesn't look or feel that way to us. It looks like all things move forward in time, it looks like the universe is an expanse of empty space populated by things, it looks like the table in front of me is solid. And because it looks that way, it is hard for us to imagine that it might be different.

What comes first, our beliefs about the way things are, or the appearance of the way things are?

Robert Lanza believes that the reason we don't perceive the reality of quantum physics is because our perception is so embedded in the paradigm of classical physics and materialism. The assumptions of the classical worldview are held so deeply in our psyche that we can't see things any other way.

We have already looked briefly at two things, the double slit experiment and quantum entanglement, that show us that reality when we look very closely, is not anything like what we think. This is not fringy science. These are not experimental results that are in question. These are results that have proven accurate for nearly a century. This is where I resonate with Lanza's passion. It's time for us to catch up with our own science. We need to be open to the fact that consciousness is not something that got added to the universe late in the game. Consciousness is an inseparable aspect of reality.

In the world of classical physics, we assume that the material universe of time and space was here first waiting for life and consciousness to arrive. We believe in the objective reality of the universe. We assume that the universe existed before there was any life or consciousness in it, and if all life and consciousness were to cease the universe would continue to exist. The subjective experience of reality is an add-on. It comes later. But how do we know this is true? Why is it so difficult to entertain a different possibility?

How do we know that yesterday exists? We have a memory of yesterday, but only that memory exists now. Now is the only moment that anyone has ever lived, so why are we so convinced of the reality of the past and the future? Remember, Einstein believed that the distinction between the past, the present, and the future was nothing but a very stubborn illusion.

If we lived in a world that was perfect as it is, maybe it would make sense to leave well enough alone, but we don't. We live in a world that is riddled with persistent problems that we don't seem able to solve. These persistent problems are one of Thomas Kuhn's indicators that a paradigm shift is needed. Many of us recognize that our world is in desperate need of massive change. We don't seem to be able to get there from where we are, and it is possible that our fundamental assumptions about reality will not allow us to get there.

There is a growing chorus of individuals from all walks of life who recognize that a paradigm shift is necessary, and given that we live in a scientific paradigm, it would seem that the revolutionary discoveries of quantum physics could be leveraged to open our minds to new possibilities and catalyze deep change.

The Enlightenment Era thinkers of Europe were born into the world of the medieval church. At that time, the priests of the church were seen as those who had privileged access to the truth. The medieval worldview began to come apart when some of its core assumptions were called into question and proven to be false. The world was not flat, the earth was not the center of the solar system, human beings were capable of thinking for themselves and understanding the laws that governed the universe. As a new understanding of reality emerged, the scientists who brought it became the new priests.

Today we are in a place where some of the fundamental assumptions of the current paradigm have been called into question. Quantum physics has already shown us that our understanding of reality is limited at best, and perhaps just plain wrong. The ground that the modern world was built on has begun to shake. The time is ripe for a paradigm shift. This shift needs volunteers, people who are willing to believe in the impossible and pioneer a new understanding of reality. I wrote this book as encouragement for those who feel this call.

> *With every advance in our scientific knowledge new elements come up, often forcing us to recast our entire picture of physical reality.*
>
> – LOUIS DE BROGLIE

Selected Bibliography

Dennett, Daniel C., *Consciousness Explained*. Back Bay Books, 1992.

Franklin, Benjamin. "*From Benjamin Franklin to Joseph Priestley, 8 February 1780*" National Archives, Founders Online, https://founders.archives.gov/documents/Franklin/01-31-02-0325

Halpern, Paul. *The Quantum Labyrinth; How Richard Feynman and John Wheeler Revolutionized Time and Reality*. Basic Books, 2017

Kuhn, Thomas S. *The Structure of Scientific Revolutions*. Enlarged 2nd ed., University of Chicago Press, 1990.

Lanza, Robert and Berman, Bob. *Biocentrism; How Life and Consciousness are the Keys to Understanding the True Nature of the Universe*. BenBella Books, 2010.

Lanza, Robert and Berman, Bob. *Beyond Biocentrism; Rethinking Time, Space, Consciousness and the Illusion of Death*. BenBella Books, 2017.

Stone, Matt and Parker, Trey. Appling. https://www.youtube.com/watch?v=vA3NLyQNDBQ

About the Author

Jeff Carreira is a meditation teacher, mystical philosopher and author who teaches to a growing number of people throughout the world. As a teacher, Jeff offers retreats and courses guiding individuals in a form of meditation he refers to as The Art of Conscious Contentment. Through this simple and effective meditation technique, Jeff has led thousands of people in the journey beyond the confines of fear and self-concern into the expansive liberated awareness that is our true home.

Ultimately, Jeff is interested in defining a new way of being in the world that will move us from our current paradigm of separation and isolation into an emerging paradigm of unity and wholeness. He is exploring some of the most revolutionary ideas and systems of thought in the domains of spirituality, consciousness, and human development. He teaches people how to question their own experience so deeply that previously held assumptions about the nature of reality fall away to create space for dramatic shifts in understanding.

Jeff is passionate about philosophy because he is passionate about the power of ideas to shape how we perceive reality and how we live together. His enthusiasm for learning is infectious, and he enjoys addressing student groups and inspiring them to develop their own powers of inquiry. He has taught students at colleges and universities throughout the world.

Jeff is the author of numerous books including:

The Art of Conscious Contentment, No Place But Home, The Miracle of Meditation, The Practice of No Problem, Embrace All That You Are, Philosophy Is Not a Luxury, Radical Inclusivity, The Soul of a New Self, and *Paradigm Shifting.*

For more about Jeff or to book him for a speaking engagement, visit: jeffcarreira.com

THE SPIRITUAL IMPLICATIONS OF QUANTUM PHYSICS

Made in United States
Troutdale, OR
08/26/2023

12376544R00056